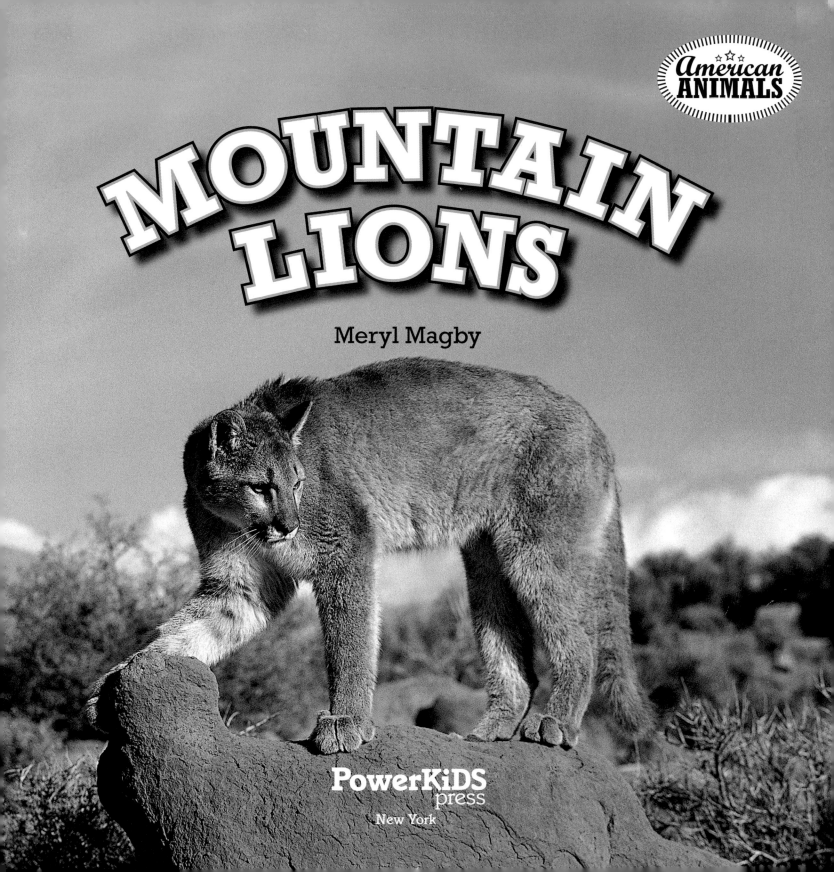

American ANIMALS

MOUNTAIN LIONS

Meryl Magby

PowerKiDS press

New York

Published in 2014 by The Rosen Publishing Group, Inc.
29 East 21st Street, New York, NY 10010

First Edition

Editor: Amelie von Zumbusch
Book Design: Ashley Drago
Layout Design: Colleen Bialecki

Photo Credits: Cover Jeremy Woodhouse/Digital Vision/Getty Images; pp. 3, 20 Hemera/ Thinkstock; p. 4 visceralimage/Shutterstock.com; pp. 5, 18 Dennis Donohue/Shutterstock.com; pp. 6, 16 Thomas Kitchin and Victoria Hurst/All Canada Photos/Getty Images; pp. 7, 8–9, 22 S. R. Maglione/ Shutterstock.com; pp. 10, 14–15, 19 (left) iStockphoto/Thinkstock; p. 11 Tom Brakefield/Photodisc/Getty Images; p. 12–13 Tom Walker/Stone/Getty Images; p. 17 Bruce Lichtenberger/Peter Arnold/Getty Images; p. 19 (top) Kane513/Shutterstock.com; p. 21 Buyenlarge/Moviepix/Getty Images.

Library of Congress Cataloging-in-Publication Data

Magby, Meryl.
 Mountain lions / by Meryl Magby. — 1st ed.
     pages cm. — (American animals)
 Includes index.
 ISBN 978-1-4777-0788-3 (library binding) — ISBN 978-1-4777-0948-1 (pbk.) — ISBN 978-1-4777-0949-8 (6-pack)
 1. Puma—Juvenile literature. I. Title.
 QL737.C23M242 2014
 599.75'24—dc23
                                        2012047576

Manufactured in the United States of America

CPSIA Compliance Information: Batch #S13PK6: For Further Information contact Rosen Publishing, New York, New York at 1-800-237-9932

Contents

North America's Lion

When you think of lions, you may think of the big yellow cats that live in Africa and Asia. However, did you know that large cats called mountain lions live in North America? In fact, they are the largest members of the cat family **native** to North America. Mountain lions are also called cougars, pumas, and panthers.

The mountain lion is known by many names, including catamount, painter, and ghost cat.

Mountain lions share an **ancestor** with the cheetah and the jaguarundi. They are also related to other cats, such as leopards, lions, and lynx, as well as the domestic cat. Mountain lions are amazing hunters. They are often the top **predators** in their **habitats**.

Unlike true lions, mountain lions cannot roar. They make many other noises, though.

From Mountains to Meadows

At one time, mountain lions could be found throughout North and South America. Today, though, their **range** in North America is much smaller. Mountain lions can be found in just sixteen states, as well as in parts of Canada and Mexico.

Different subspecies, or kinds, of mountain lions live in different places. For example, Florida panthers live in the swamps and forests of southern Florida.

Mountain lions can live in many different habitats. These include high mountains, dry deserts, wet swamps, dark forests, and green meadows. However, mountain lions must live in places where they can easily find animals to eat. They also need hiding places for hunting, sleeping, and protecting their babies. Mountain lions do not like to live in places where there are lots of people.

This mountain lion is in Montana. Most of the mountain lions in Montana live in the state's mountains and foothills.

Amazing Eyes and Ears

Mountain lions have short fur coats that are tan on top and white underneath. The tips of their tails and ears are black. Adult mountain lions generally weigh between 75 and 175 pounds (34–79 kg). Their bodies are around 8 feet (2.4 m) long from nose to tail. They stand about 30 inches (76 cm) tall at the shoulder.

> The color of a mountain lion's fur varies slightly from animal to animal, but they are always some shade of tan.

Mountain lions have excellent eyesight. Their large yellow eyes have **adapted** to see very well in the dark. This is important because they hunt at night. Mountain lions also have amazing hearing. They can hear **high-frequency** sounds that tell them where other animals are quietly hiding.

Powerful Jaws and Claws

Mountain lions are carnivores. This means they eat only meat. Deer is the mountain lion's favorite food. They also eat other wild animals such as elk, squirrels, rabbits, skunks, porcupine, birds, and mice.

Mountain lions sometimes attack livestock and pets when they cannot find wild animals to hunt. They very rarely attack people.

Mountain lions hunt by hiding until their **prey** wanders by. Then, they quietly stalk the animal before jumping on it. They use their sharp claws to hook their prey and then bite its neck with their powerful jaws. Mountain lions generally do not eat big kills in one meal. They drag their leftovers to a hiding place and cover them up. They come back to eat the rest later.

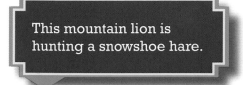

This mountain lion is hunting a snowshoe hare.

Mountain Lion Facts

1. Mountain lions may live up to 13 years in the wild. However, many only live to be about 6 years old.

2. The largest mountain lion ever found by humans weighed 276 pounds (125 kg).

3. Although they have amazing sight and hearing, mountain lions do not have a very good sense of smell.

4. A mountain lion's tail is about one-third the length of its body, or around 2.5 feet (0.8 m) long.

5. Their large paws make it easy for mountain lions to chase other animals over deep snow.

6. Mountain lion tracks are sometimes mistaken for dog or bobcat tracks. However, mountain lions have teardrop-shaped toes, unlike the oval-shaped toes of dogs and bobcats.

7. Male mountain lions are generally larger than female mountain lions.

8. One mountain lion may kill about 35 deer a year.

Marking and Mating

Mountain lions are **territorial**. They live alone for most of the year and protect their territory from other mountain lions. However, a male's territory may overlap with those of several females. Mountain lions mark their territory with claw marks on trees and the smell of their urine.

> A mountain lion's territory can be between 10 and 785 square miles (26–2,033 sq km). Males and mountain lions that live in places where food is hard to find have larger territories.

Male and female mountain lions may **mate** at any time of the year. Females make loud screaming noises to attract a mate. The male and female spend a few days together hunting and playing before they mate. Then, they go their separate ways. After about three months, the female finds a den to have her babies, called kittens.

Kittens Growing Up

Mountain lion kittens weigh about one pound (0.5 kg) when they are born. They have blue eyes and spotted fur. The kittens drink their mother's milk, which helps them to grow quickly. After about eight weeks, they weigh 30 pounds (14 kg).

Mountain lion mothers most often have two to three kittens at a time.

Mountain lion kittens start eating meat when they are about six weeks old. The mother protects her kittens from predators and teaches them to hunt. Their spots disappear by the time they are a year old. Their eyes turn yellow soon after. After 18 months, kittens leave their mothers. Life can be hard for young mountain lions. They have more predators than adults do.

These mountain lion kittens are staying at their den while their mother is out hunting.

Very Few Predators

Unlike some other predators, mountain lions are good at climbing trees and will do so to protect themselves.

Adult mountain lions do not have many natural predators. This is because they are stronger, faster, or bigger than other predators in their habitats. Mountain lions also have many **defenses**. Their excellent hearing and night vision let them know when other animals are nearby. They can also use their sharp claws to protect themselves. Mountain lions can jump 20 feet (6 m) up into the air and leap 40 feet (12 m) on the ground.

However, wolves and bears sometimes kill mountain lions, especially young or sick ones. Older mountain lions may kill younger ones looking for food or water in their territory.

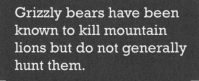

Grizzly bears have been known to kill mountain lions but do not generally hunt them.

Mountain lions also defend themselves with their sharp teeth and powerful jaws.

People and Mountain Lions

Mountain lions lived throughout North America before European settlers came. Most Native Americans rarely hunted mountain lions. However, the new settlers were afraid they would attack people and livestock. They began hunting mountain lions. As more land was settled, the mountain lions' habitats shrank.

Mountain lions had a special role in the spiritual beliefs of some Native American peoples. Others did not hunt them because there were easier animals to hunt.

In some early American settlements, **bounties** were put on mountain lions. This means that hunters were paid for each mountain lion they killed. States continued to put bounties on mountain lions until the twentieth century. By the 1850s, mountain lions were dying out in eastern and midwestern states. They were becoming rare in western states as well.

For many years, Americans thought of mountain lions mainly as dangerous animals, as you can see in this movie poster from 1932.

21

Keeping Mountain Lions Safe

Today, there are about 30,000 mountain lions in the United States. In some states, hunters are still allowed to kill small numbers of mountain lions each year. In other states, hunting mountain lions is illegal.

Conservation groups are working to keep mountain lions and their habitats safe. They hope that the number of mountain lions in the United States will grow much larger as time goes by. If you visit a national park in the western United States, you may even be lucky enough to see a mountain lion!

This beautiful mountain lion is in Utah's Zion National Park.

Glossary

adapted (uh-DAP-ted) Changed to fit requirements.

ancestor (AN-ses-ter) A relative who lived long ago.

bounties (BOWN-teez) Payment for killing animals or criminals.

conservation (kon-sur-VAY-shun) Keeping something safe.

defenses (DEE-fents-ez) Things a living thing does that help keep it safe.

habitats (HA-buh-tats) The kinds of land where animals or plants naturally live.

high-frequency (HY-FREE-kwen-see) Having a high sound.

mate (MAYT) To come together to make babies.

native (NAY-tiv) Born or grown in a certain place or country.

predators (PREH-duh-terz) Animals that kill other animals for food.

prey (PRAY) An animal that is hunted by another animal for food.

range (RAYNJ) The places in which a kind of animal can be found.

territorial (ter-uh-TAWR-ee-ul) Guarding land or space for one's own use.

Index

Websites

Due to the changing nature of Internet links, PowerKids Press has developed an online list of websites related to the subject of this book. This site is updated regularly. Please use this link to access the list:

www.powerkidslinks.com/amer/lion/